Werewolves Don't Celebrate Hanukkah

By Michelle Franklin

Werewolves choreographed by Jonathan Burrello

*I was told to leave this page blank, for werewolf reasons.

For Myndil, Aodhgan, and Eochaid.

For Dr. Kaja Franck, Dr. Emily Zarka, and all those who love good boy werewolves.

For everyone on Twitter, who wouldn't read my last book, so I had to write this one.

*I had to leave this page blank also, to give the werewolves time to take their places. It's hard work posing for holiday photos. Props and staging are paramount.

Werewolves don't celebrate Hanukkah.

This is a shame, because they would be rather good at it.

They would be perfect for welcoming the holiday, because Hanukkah begins at night. They could announce the holiday with a howl at sundown, and do an additional howl for every subsequent night, *making eight howls on the last night to honour all eight nights.

*They like doing this in succession, because while they have the urge to do all eight howls at once, howling at the same time causes arguments, and quibbles simply won't do among werewolves.

They would be great at making latkes, because they come with natural potato peelers. Long claws also make great wedges and fries. They would have to call friends to help with the onions, but this is a small sacrifice they're willing to make for the sake of fried potatoes.

They would be perfect for preparing desserts because they love doughnuts. This is not just a werewolf custom; everyone loves doughnuts in some form or other, especially ones with custard filling. Werewolves prefer their doughnuts jam-filled, because they cannot have chocolate. Some believe that werewolves can eat chocolate in their human forms, but many are afraid to test this, so no one has tried.

They would be expert at sniffing out fake Hanukkah gelt. All the chocolate coins would go to the children, all the money would go to the townspeople, and the werewolves would get treats for doing a great job, because good boys and girls are always rewarded during the holiday.

Pats on the head are also accepted.

They would be adept at playing dreidel. They would have to spin the dreidel in their human forms, but once the dreidel is spinning, the werewolves could chase it round in circles, which they're used to doing, because they often chase their long fluffy tails.

They could gather round the spinning dreidel with their bevy of canine cousins and take bets on which of those going in circles should fall over first:

werewolf or dreidel?

They would be proficient at singing songs. They would bray out Ma'oz Tzur on key, unlike most humans. They would also sing every stanza of the song, instead of getting tired after singing only the first stanza, also unlike most humans.

The song does talk about *'defeating barking foes' after all.

*There were werewolves around when the song was written, but the song is not about them. Perhaps it was written *by* a werewolf, which would make sense.

They could help light the Hanukkah candles. They would have to light the menorah in their human forms, but they would make sure that everyone put the candles in from right to left and light them from left to right.

Werewolves have better sense and directional awareness than most people.

They would make the best gift givers, because their thick fur is perfect for hiding small presents in. Wrapping paper is probably their *greatest enemy, because their claws are always getting in the way, but they do make perfectly curly ribbons.

*Socks are actually their greatest enemy, but not on purpose; socks have no agenda but to keep feet warm, and werewolves come with warm feet attached. Hanukkah is the international day of sock-exchange. Socks make popular gifts because everyone needs them, except werewolves, who slice through the toe bits with their claws. Werewolves love Hanukkah, but not enough to do socks about it.

They might have difficulty saying '*Chag Sameakh!' in their wolf forms, but they can growl, which is nearly the same thing. They can also do big howls or small ones on command. The big awoos! are how they say "Happy Hanukkah!" in werewolf.

Coincidentally, this is also how they say 'I'm hungry' and 'Go away', just like Bubbeh Yenta when she makes indistinct grunts.

*[χagsaˈme.aχ] for linguists. For all other humans: khahg sahmei-akh.

They would settle the debate over which way the word should be spelled: Chanukkah, Hanukkah, Hannuka, Chanukah, Hanuka—but they would each choose a spelling and have gripping wrestling matches over it. The winner among them would declare their chosen spelling the superlative forever, so everyone would know how to spell it when making out their cards, and if someone should say, "That's not how it's spelled!" you could just point to the werewolf who won and say, "Take it up with them."

They would make amazing dinner guests. They would bring their own werewolf dishes out of politeness; they're connoisseurs of fine meat and understand about brisket. They also clean their own plates by licking them, and they never overstay their welcome, knowing that it's time to go home when the moon yawns and the stars begin to wink themselves to sleep.

They also understand about miracles. Their transformations are miraculous and certainly more exciting than Bubbeh Yenta's *kugel, because most things are. Even more miraculous is how they've been able to survive through the ages on brisket. Their ancestors may or may not have been among the Maccabees for the rededication of the Second Temple, but they think Yahudah HaMakabi, Judah the Hammer, is a wonderful name, and the rebellion that led to the Maccabee victory was quite miraculous.

*Bubbeh Yenta still being alive after last year's kugel incident is also a miracle.

Werewolves don't celebrate Chanukkah, but there is time to rectify that.

They already celebrate a similar Festival of Lights, one that honours the night sky, glories in the light hiding behind the moon, and celebrates the brocade of stars strung across a celestial loom.

They would be glad to join your celebrations, so put a plate aside for them and save the doughnuts for when they arrive. They might hulk and growl and bare their fangs, but they'll be happy, unlike Bubbeh Yenta, who also hulks and growls and never smiles, but gives you presents anyway.

Awoo!

(Werewolf translation: Happy *Hanukkah!)

*This is the spelling that was decided upon by the werewolf wrestling. I had originally spelled it Channukah, because that's how I've been spelling it since I was a child, but then the Hanukkah werewolf won, so this is how we have to spell it now. Or else.

Draw your own werewolves celebrating Hanukkah!

Give the werewolves names and share them with us over social media!

Or else.

Michelle Franklin is the author of twenty-five other fantasy and nonfiction books you should absolutely read, including The Misadventures of Myndil Plodostirr, Frewyn Fables, and the Introvert series.

Jonathan Burrello is the cartoonist and illustrator behind hundreds of comics and webtoons, including Barb and Haunted Safari. He also loves terrible films and is happy about it.